THE C₀INSPIRATOR

Anthology of The Bent Mast Poets

2019

To Alain ¿ Valerie,
Cheers,
Celso
Dec 3, 2019

Bull Kelp Books

VICTORIA

THE CoINSPIRATOR, Volume 1
First Edition. Published November 2019.
© 2019 by Bull Kelp Books, Victoria, BC, Canada
bullkelpbooks.com

~

EDITOR: Poems selected and edited by the authors
DESIGN AND PRODUCTION: Jerome Ashmore Peacock
ART: Photos and illustrations are original works by the contributors

~

THE CoINSPIRATOR, published annually, is an independent anthology of poetry by The Bent Mast Poets, Victoria, BC Canada. This is the inaugural volume. All rights reserved by the authors and contributors. All poems are works of the imagination. Bull Kelp Books, *THE CoINSPIRATOR*, and The Bent Mast Poets are protected trademarks.

Special thanks to: the Victoria Creative Writing Group for its support and The Bent Mast Pub for providing a fine place to imbibe and co-inspire.

Contents

Poets Gathering

Historical Victorian the perfect location
Its name the Bent Mast
An ale house full of energy
Awaits the poets' inspiration

The room is quiet
One more sip or maybe two
Now your turn, take a deep breath
'Tis the command you pursue

Wonderful words capture a moment
Some spiritual, some sad
Some of beauty
Some a little bold, naughty or bad

Listen closely, imagination has no end
Not asking for approval
Just hoping you'll relate
And together transcend.

NANHA

Madeira, Grapes with a Wreath, nnn...
No Wrath

Color lends to the squished
acidity to wrap the tongue
each time every time
an expectation
aged vintaged
barreled and Bacchus fermented
Final vessels glassy & crystalline
prior to the palate being teased

Meandering as inebriated
prepare to hand over reins
in percentage
to Eros(love) , Ares (war) and simpleton buffoonery
(I have embraced her with open arms but I can't name her)
in parts
Spirits as reformist filters
they Manifest faults

But not for me
fruity ether as suffrage
is an assist to daydreams
In them I have been
many beings
I am not

In turns
Gargantuan, better hung
electric to touch, luminescent,
shimmering in heat,
perpetually aroused.
it's all about having the organ
imaginably Cocked

another turn
bacchanalian dreams string them up

I am the bluish planet
Water covered orb
in resplendent splendor
circling the burning yellow ogre
The alpha I spin to
but a dance with my lassoed beta,
silvery satellite on the side
whooshes a rhythmic tidal slosh
Awash my nether parts,
ugh, uh, ah
My skirts in a furl
Triangulation complete
functional ménage à trois
waltz in elliptical swings
cyclic & unending wetting of parts
yo ho king tides are a hit

into another turn
I see me as puff pastry
Shutter me with lips, savory!
perky sweetness floats up
some content sinks
My effervescence
is yet
some kitty's pagan fluffy itty bits
delectable

bacchanalian dreams are sensate
once bottled content is gobbled up
ultimate self fellatio
Beautifulls hop me
Hops on hops
Don't stop
Pour till I drop

Ajit

Shelter Sans Shade

dedicated to the missing indigenous women

Wont' let today be a yesterday

first born to the land/nation
how could the land lay waste the
claim to me?

The squalor is hidden too often
the verbose of squalor was taught strange, once created do not
    clear
lay bare the burrow
just dig another.

Food on the table simply pushed aside, expect a new plate
which may be gleamed or not clear the table, nasty microbes
deserve a treat.

Taken and schooled in shame foreign to
my creed
ingrained skin deep, delved and
shoveled almost into the genes
for some decades past
now hard to to live down the prepubescent
hubris
the skeletal shell is hunched low
the shoulders slack.

Released to navigate, innards paradox(ed) rife
uncertainty surfaces in each stride
spirits try to guide, yet demons now have a king
which the collars inscribed
couple of generations asunder, completely missing a guide

expectation unknown, performance here and now
mimic, please, simply wander
step in , step out, maybe crash any couch sufficed

The crusader knights
with the straighter posture
lean in
the innuendo is now sexual, peaks

roadsides, fields, car seats I occupied
frayed aimless before any start

curves that excite denigrate
when priced, how? When? Why?
Did I?!

imagery in my brainstorm reeks
chagrin clouded orgasm it still seeks
there is substance in multiplicity
procured on streets, alleviates
the vex, moments of shelter
knowing no real shade.

Ecstasy mars orgasm, articulated nonsensical
double positives cancel out, just the same as double negatives

I am hung dry, hit upon
hit on,
shot, strangulated
bashed to sieve the body from soul
some type of hunger fulfilled
not mine
aberrant societal bred, never in check

now missing, no frenzy in the search
search without commitment
the carcass a minority
a vote bank that requisitions no lobby

remains scattered, pockmarked nation
each spot seeks a marker, a familial name,
closure,
for those who wait

anonymity as perpetuity for some assured
not labor but luck leads a few home

a moment when I (some) can say goodbye, time lapsed,
poignant still as ash or bone lovingly glanced,
they see the earth covering the wreck.
a repeated moment, a human moment,
I wanted to be kissed goodbye,
false, false, utterly false; even the end lacks.

spectator commentates speculating on some of
her last thoughts
to her adoptive
father/mother/unified confederation/guardian potentate/shelter
unlikely though thru fear and terror but still

"don't let today be yesterday."

Ajit

Learning to Feel

Somewhere along the way,
I learned to breath thru the skin.
Oxygenated in a new way.

This way I could feel.

The scabbard of skin sheathing the soul
enabling nourishment.
Cheek and jaw touching softness,
inhaling in smells not registered
in nostrils,
coursing in the blood reaching
the brain with the
'you' flavored breath.

Madhosh, intoxicated to the brim
giddy settling thoughts.

Spark gap diminished,
rubberized fireband wherever we touch.
Syncing hastened blood beats,
exchanging lassoed in
non-gaseous air.
Ensnared poignant fragrance,
essence of you, not sucked but scrubbed in.

It comes and goes, this breath thru the skin.
Which is the keepsake
the memory or the skin borne breath.

Amulets and scarabs are out there
worn by living ones, touching skin
captured whiffs, essence
of skin felt effervescence
of living breath.

Ajit

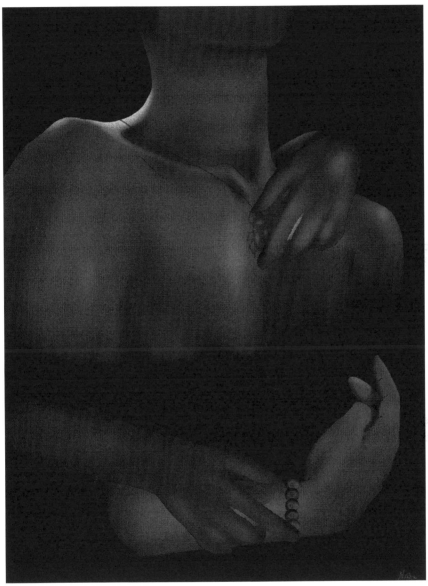

NANHA

Osiris

the flames of war drip on the innocent,
the global power, all knowing
who, and where.

the terrorist, his own Osiris,
knife in hand, his crook,
voice so low it soothes,
as innocents
dig their canopic jar.

my cry,
impotent,
unheard,
blind to images
like fingerprints,
frame by frame
yellow buildings, now dust.

the light gives time,
footprints in the sand
fade as the Benben stone.
here Babbage and Turing
your math now music,
colossal, deciphering the mystery of death,
Osiris crumbles.

my gods of science,
my gods of brilliance,
you can find us,
stop the cry.
Osiris, have I let you steal my future?

Lynn D. Baron

Grains of Sand

against the indigo sky,
beneath the slip of a moon,
cloaked in the dark of lamp smoke
in the arms of angels,
home came to God.

whispers crossed time, land and sea,
a mass of raven black curls,
the little girl, on sand,
like icing sugar ,
buckets of seawater by her side,
tiny hands sculpt and shape
the grains of sand ,
her cathedral to the stars.

God,
not in a hurry ,
watches and smiles
as water drips and grains of sand stick,
in praise to the wind and the water,
the earth and the sky.

Lynn D. Baron

Bella

bella
shiny threads of spider silk
circle her heart,
burn like coal
wild upon the marble floor.

ashes,
grey ashes
black ashes
quiet and still,
burning keys
open golden doors now charred,
and backroads close like night.

ashes,
softly, gently
tears bind them
soft lips kiss them
softly , gently,
charred hands caress them,
shapes them.
and slowly,
ash by ash
bella returns

Lynn D. Baron

Contagion

relentless,
like waves against the garden wall,
sun warms the sea
and stars ignite water.
fealty clings like pathos,
another jewel bought.
tears wash his face,
no truer today than yesterday,
too late for high praise,
there are many more that Cupid
with his arrow, kills.
eat them.

Lynn D. Baron

Frame

he climbs the stairs
slowly,
the rail gripped firmly in his hand,
the carpet, once the color of wheat in spring,
now white,
worn.

stops,
his blue eyes clouded with age
scans the side board
and he thinks of long hours spent wandering,
yesterday, among the trees in the park,
alone.

he walks to the chair,
velvet brocade, faded by sun,
misshappened cushions, flattened ,
invite him warmly

he reaches for the picture
framed in silver, tarnished with age,
like him.
he smiles
as fingers brush the surface of glass
a woman, smiling,
a forest at her back.

slowly
deliberately,
he swallows,
white,
whole,
easily,
one at a time,
gnarled hands hold the silver frame.

Lynn D. Baron

Pursuit of the Poet

Eternal days and black skies
fill with blotted and chaotic words,
foaming,
moulding,
concealed among the clouds.
gagged and bound,
gasp for words suspended
hidden within a dim ray of light
bring magic,
intent so deep,
it's water.

Lynn D. Baron

tart

you taste of vinegar, ash, and cinnamon
with a lick of despair around the edges
which is probably why i like you so much

Hugh Blackthorne

HUGH BLACKTHORNE

slither

slide and slip
between soft grasses,
rough thorns
against my glide
i curl along
your bloodied boots
pacing dry leaves
over parched soil
Day passes, watching
you turn to dust, while
i am caught amid
vine and shadows
and then you draw
shut the oak door
over the looking glass
reflecting us
i press down,
make narrow tracks
into cold earth
to creep from view
down here, alone,
I find the dark night
and try to forget
your brightest star.

Hugh Blackthorne

HUGH BLACKTHORNE

the things you left behind

digital debris clutters
desktops virtual and real
stacks of half-written works
and ephemeral sketches
imprisoned in notebooks
and unreliable devices
while your ghost riots
over battered velvet
and tendrils of poetry
with roots in decay
leaves scratch daylight
cracking the spine
of lazy afternoons
feathered taxidermy
to take flight
but most of all
you've left the static
hiss of your mysteries
so loud and so bright
i have to turn away
because that glow
burns electric
searing my skin—
together we share neon
madness, rampant in spring

Hugh Blackthorne

HUGH BLACKTHORNE

do you remember?

that time tea travelled to me by ups,
state by state, across a continent
to swirl fuchsia blooms
in my mug, summer caught
on my tongue, in my teeth
take that taste, my summer-twin,
turned grief, turned loss,
my dwelling-place crafted
in a nest of twigs and twine,
to make a space of memory
which plays like tricksters,
hard muscle-memory cramps,
down with the moss and grass,
in my dirt tea-house amid worms
and a scrape of herbal offerings
for everything that ails us,
a poultice applied for grief
and love, the same thing really,
or maybe a tourniquet to staunch
the bleeding from a torn flesh
wound that puckers sour,
like lemon ginger, out here lost
in mossy rocks and broken
bricks, where ghosts dig in,
and haunt the pair of us.

Hugh Blackthorne

HUGH BLACKTHORNE

the sea, the sea

Farmer to Sea: "Your waves sink ships."
Sea to Farmer: "The wind makes waves, not me."
Aesop

Our Father who art in Heaven
hallowed be thy name...
religion is like water—
you drink
and
silently
alpha to omega
panta rhei.
Windmills turn
dykes stop sea
and
silently
polders drain
and tulips grow.
Arab Spring!
Orontes bursts its banks
and
silently
hijabs trip over clogs
and minarets tilt at windmills.
There is no god but God
and Muhammad is his Prophet.

Paul G. Chamberlain

A Dark Tale

For I.B.

All is silent...

Knight stands on beach.

Shadow appears.

I have been waiting for you
says Knight.
I have been following you
replies Shadow.
I want more time
says Knight.
They all say that
says Shadow.

A game:—

Is there life after death?
asks Knight
moving his white Pawn.

I cannot say
Shadow replies
moving his black Pawn.

Tell me there is Heaven!
exclaims Knight.

Can you not hear the cries of the Trojan Women?
Shadow asks.

I hear only wind and water
replies Knight.

Beyond the hill is famine
says Shadow.
All have fled save two.
As we play our game for time
a fair maid is being tupped by a priest—
will God pardon him for his tale?

Is there nothing that can be done?
asks Knight.

Nothing.

Why is Python circling Parnassus?
Knight asks.

The Dance of Death
says Shadow.
A sad procession:
a dwarf carries a wooden cross
a hag whips a hunchback, and
a priest waves incense
to ward off pestilence.

Is there nothing that can be done?
asks Knight.

Nothing.

What is the black smoke beyond the hill?
Knight asks.

A maid of Orleans:
She confessed to priests wielding the malleus maleficarum.
Her soul is being cleansed by fire.

Is there nothing that can be done?
asks Knight.

Nothing.

What is wrong with my world?
asks Knight.

You must see life as it is
says Shadow:
revel in wine, women and song
hug your wife and embrace your child.
The world is all that is—that is all.

I will go to my castle beyond the mountains
announces Knight.

Too late!
smiles Shadow
taking Knight's King.
Our little jest is over.

The Seventh Seal opens—

All is silent.

Paul G. Chamberlain

Oberiuty

*"I am interested only in nonsense; only in that which makes no
practical sense. I am interested in life in its absurd manifestation."*
daniil kharms

Imagine the sun as God, the Earth as the Son, and gravity as
the Holy Spirit...now imagine Tycho Brahe probing the universe
with an infinitely long telescope, discovering another Earth, a
mirror image of our own, where bicycles ride on water, water
turns into sunshine, and people rise from the dead. Imagine all
this.

Now forget it.

W4M:—
Mona (not your average Lisa)
looking for picture with frame
easel not necessary
will mount.

Paul G. Chamberlain

Les Dunn

They found Les sprawled in his lazy chair
Long grass spiked up past his elbows
Arms stiffly down, fingers scratching the ground
But only when the rain blew in, slanting from the north
Ants found footholds between his fingers and the stale doritos
That washed off his chest in the weeks that passed
They ran over his wristwatch and up past his shoulders
Looking for tasty pieces that came away easily.

Les used to play the drums while popping Quaaludes
Hitting the snare in the same place until it broke
He did best on the slow songs with the brushes
"Wings of a Dove," or "Sentimental Journey."
The night life and drugs drove him flabby and grim
So he gave up music for the lazy chair.

Yes, he loved that lazy chair,
Long and wide, sagging close to the earth.
Wouldn't even split it with his ex-wife
She received the car instead.
"That's not a good deal," said his friends
Les smiled and popped another pill
"I'm comfy enough," he replied,
As he stupored through the days,
Dreaming he was back with the band
Beating out "Who'll stop the Rain" in some Legion Hall

Spiders skitter up the trailer walls
In the folds of his beard, they spin their webs.

Kim Harrison

Poem 101

Twenty empty snuff cans
Full of powerful tiny roaches
Several packs of chocolate bars
Melting slowly near the fireplace

Man lights a cigarette
Different one from yesterday
Dog laps at a bowl of beer
On a three legged couch stands a half full bottle

Man's fingers scratched and dirt embedded
Moving scissors back and forth
Carving thick white guitar picks
From discarded plastic jugs

Then Man grabs a two string guitar
From atop some wood stacked in the hallway
Tunes the strings to make a sound
One drone one key one buzz

Dog licks the bowl quite clean, lies
Waiting for a chocolate bar
Windows wet with morning rain
Man stands playing at the doorway

Kim Harrison

Poem 102

On the graveyard shift
A man walked off the sawmill roof
Quite by accident
Looking up
To see what mattered
He dodged a snowman
Plunging from the sky

Both the snowman and he
Crash-landed in an open rail car
Conveniently located below the flat roof
And luckily filled with soft aspen wood chips

The man stood up
Wiped snow from his eyes
And wood from his shoes
Munched a chocolate covered carrot
Dropped all the way from Alpha Centauri

It was early July
Light already returning
Filling space once full of stars

Kim Harrison

Antisocial Sign Disorder

Walk on the grass feed the bears smoke on bus trespass here
trample underbrush throw litter in sea don't recycle cans talk
    in library sleep on subway spit in pool do not line up be a
    contrary fool
Chaos will result if there are no signs
Just by themselves they keep us in line
So many of us with our human natures
Everyone checking out the nomenclature
Most obey but a few ignore
Stone age to sign age super ego id war
It's easy to dis what the writing commands
But if we don't follow . . . it'll get out of hand
Get out of hand get out of hand
Dog excrement in a playground zone
You're with your pooch and you hear the phone
ring ring don't pick it up ring ring
don't pick it up
hello hello we're having fun
crypto cryptosporidium
run on walk way walk on run way
spin in stuck place stick in spin race
kick it in yeah kick it in
it's a crowded world kick it in
park in zone reserved for the handicapped
contrary zone can't find it on a road map
text it text it now text it text it now
throw litter in lake jaywalk here
give verbal abuse let pit bulls loose
eat with no shirt eat with no shoes eat with no pants just chew
    chew chew I demand service I demand service service service
    I demand service
i pod on at heart operation
do I perceive doctor irritation?
School zone speed up work zone speed up play zone speed up
    any zone speed up speed up speed up
Bike on sidewalk Bike in mall Bike in hospital Bike thru wall
Contrary zone ride ride Contrary zone ride ride

Kim Harrison

Am I Too Big?

Am I too big
Will I fit in?
Or will I explode
Like a big truckload?

I've got big hands
And I've got big feet
I've got a trunk like an elephant
What a giant freak!
I can't get out
And I can't get in
My face is so huge
I'm a movie screen
Getting so close now
hear the audience scream

Got a big house
Though it's mostly air
Got big wheels
Can't find a spare
Got a big handshake hello hello hello
When I wave goodbye
A hurricane blows

It's unfortunate
I can't proportion it
An awesome sight
of the greatest might
And I can't get through
cause I'm bigger than you

Too big too big mighty large humungous
Stuck in between two places
making a big rumpus

Am I too big?
Will I fit in?
Or will I explode
Like a big truck load?

Kim Harrison

Eye and Centre

I thought I could keep you from crashing but no. I'm just the
nose dive co-pilot. I said maybe we could make this better and so
 you
increased direct flights to the quay of Malcontent. Nothing
good ever happens there. And we languish for weeks
in the ultra violet radiation of your anger. There's no
support coming. This is an emergency. Ok
so you are an island and after your hurricane, nothing
is open. Everything has been emptied, evacuated.
Steel doors come down like they do in the third world
so nothing gets in and I just stand outside
and spray graffiti on your eyelids. I get it. This is your rebellion—
a form of Independence. Wave your flag from a balcony
that is still above water. There is debris everywhere. Dishes
smashed, a cutting board thrown through the wall
and the lights have come on. You are a man on the roof
shouting with your arms for someone to save you
while warm water pours in the windows. I go
through the motions, throw the rope. I get
so fucking hungry I forget who I am. I just want to
sit down across from you at a restaurant
and rub your cock under the table
with my bare feet. Bring something back to life.
But under these circumstances
there is nothing to survive on just lightening
and blues roots, and then
the suck of the undertow.

Joelene Heathcote

Love

First there was the leaving.
And the leaving, a grey turning—cold as the spit
of desolation. And there is her stillness too, her naked body
calling him back to the bed's white apology, a treading
of water, a conversation with loss that has been
the slamming of doors, a way of walking
before even legs.

And before the leaving there was crawling, there were
words on their knees, crippled or hopeless as days of rainfall.
Days and nights of mouthing the soft things he wanted,
tasting what he thought he could not live without. And at
breakfast he brought it to her. The leaving, sticking
to the roof of his mouth, dry as a tongue full of feathers.
Something had broken its neck and lay, the way truth does,
as if sleeping by the front door.

Maybe the river of woe is as good a place as any to let her down.
Good enough for plucking the coin from her eyes
and flipping it between them. The high-noted ting
of its falling against metal, or wood-frame, its steel-toothed
hummingbird frequency. Then heads, you lose.

And he thought about it in the pub, a decent place
to talk. But when his mouth opened ruin spilled, ash—
all the things he had killed, the tiny bones, and the fur,
and the heart of it. He had done it out of habit, as a test,
because something inside him needed praying for.

And his mouth pinned like a poppy at the centre of his face,
blistered when he said the word leaving like you could
put something down that simply and when
he said it what he said was the breaking of glass
and laughter in a collection plate of fuck yous. And he
knew now the difference between want and need. And
leaving was easier than squeezing what he really wanted
from the tight opening of his throat.

Joelene Heathcote

Ori, Means Folding

You think this has no expiration date, it does. See it says right here, Fuck you. No one needs to feel guilty for loving. It's not just a weakness like Deep n' Delicious. It's not just synthetic though in your world synthetic is synonymous with good enough if you spit on it. You are a door closing, locked. There is someone on the other side on her knees. You know that. She's Origami folded into a Lotus, like something enlightened. Don't look at what is being lost. Search girls eating pussy—something nubile as bubble gum on a window. Put your sunglasses on, and cradle your dick in your palm. Just keep running.

Joelene Heathcote

Machinery

If you can hear the pussy in her voice you'll stay on the line.
Put up with any incompetence just to hear what bewilderment
sounds like in a French accent or East Indian—the best of both
    worlds
on technical support. She has just woken up or she has a cold. She
    is cold.
Look at her nipples. Her ping is high but her hair is thick
and tousled, has been curled by sleep. Oh, she's rolling toward you
in the bed and her ass is impossibly smooth—something crème
Anglais. Unplug your router. Plug it back in.
This is her first time. She's all joy. She's
so patient. She's licking your balls with her voice.

This is what you've been missing. Stay on the line.
A little girl is lost on the edge of customer service. She needs
a taxi back to your hotel room. She's someone trapped but
still breathing—a risk
but you have always been a hero. Don't forget that.
The old you is around here
somewhere—in the driver's seat. You're pulling up
in a yellow car and she's opening
your passenger door. Her leg is inside and above
the rain wet panties—you move
your mouth up the backs of her thighs
and then closer. Get closer, tap on it.
Speak into the microphone.

Joelene Heathcote

Mnemonics for a Pair of Hands

When I touch your face it is the only way my fingers have
of speaking. It's their first time believing
in anything, the first touching
of something this perfect. Never accuse them
of insincerity because truth is the only
language they know. I like to think they have

salt in themselves, that they are ten disciples
on the river bank of remembering and if even

you thought they were lying, they could never
cross, could never be or become anything beautiful again.

The idea of fingertips seeing is something someone
should have thought of a long time ago: their collective
past life—a personal history of touching that has been tattooed
on their faces like a footprint in a Zen sand garden. Maybe
that form of meditation is in some way akin to this
tactile transmigration. Maybe the tips of my fingers
have raked the world and been tamed, and spoken
gently with the heart. I like that—the notion that they might
have found you by themselves through many incarnations,
over time, just as wind-blown plum blossoms
might do

Sometimes they see themselves
as just that, having the soul of
pink petals hand blown across your pathway,
becoming winged again, living as a soft whisper
of wind in a meadow that will taxi in
the slow incinerated dark

Once upon a time my entire hands were birds
that had bathed in the waters of Lethe
and then broken their pearly necks
against everything they thought was straight

and clear and so

they have spent a long time burning
in the papillary ridges
of an underworld

I want to believe they've
done their time now—linguists
of sorrow and ecstasy and beauty
what purity is left of them migrates over every
instantiation like scarlet feathers, like confetti

To say they have sinned is simplistic
All this time they have been looking for you.
They have wandered, and hungered and
though they ate they were never anything other
than ordinary fingers on what appeared to be an ordinary hand
cupped like a useless bowl that had never held anything
that filled them.

Joelene Heathcote

A Reality Check

Here, the rhythm never changes,
the ebb and flow of timeless tides,
by moonlight or the dark of night,
roll in and out long before the sundial.
Seagulls and other eyes, pacing
the next incoming with great expectations.

Crawling out of my sleeping chamber
into my brothers' body odors,
homeless, dressed for hunger.
Stigmatized as such, but I am not,
didn't crash land in area 51,
homeless in my home, (planet) not quite.

Out of the grand lodge, they kicked me
because, to their Gods, I wouldn't submit.
Ever since my LSD haze,
my conscience drowned in reality.
Now I can see the tree for its being,
delight in Dharma, seek its meaning.

In the Petri dish of humanity,
blooms the celestial reflection
of unconscious existence.
Oh, strange lover, daughter of Google,
why must you know, where and when
I last visited the outhouse.

Feathered wings skyward swing.
The winds of change are picking up,
ominous cracks glow on a dark horizon.
In the depth of debt, an explosion,
vibrating humanity back into reality.
At a different rhythm, the continuum continues.

Dieter Hettstedt

As the Sun Rises

A working woodpecker woke me
early this morning.
I could have dreamed longer,
but after you rolled me over,
while the tent was flapping,
passion drove me to explore further.

The waterfall,
spraying purity in my face,
mesmerizing my senses,
I became a loafer and followed
the path of enlightenment
through twin peaked mountains,
into the streaming river valley,
erecting lifesaving protection
before the dam will burst,
releasing a fresh squad
of spawning salmons.

After smelling the roses
and kissing the navel,
a ray of sunshine
falling through a pair of living trees,
from which a hairy night owl
looked at me,
reflecting the beauty to be had.
It's time to recharge my desires
for further engagements.

Dieter Hettstedt

Mirage

Looking in your eyes,
down deep - the universe;
heat vents on the ocean floor,
spew eternity;
a spark in your eye - recycled,
like soulmates on the same wave;
salty microplastics reflect
the reality of the day;
our immortal souls, on a different
level of unreality,
floating in a parallel delta;
are we all of one or
am I the only one
who sees the stars
for what they are, cold, far, tempting
and in the mind's eye only ?

In my vision,
you reflect the unexplained;
I feel your inner being,
the vibration of my frequencies;
yet, I cannot read you
but I know you
like a cedar tree knows its root
or the ocean waves know the wind.
in resonance, entanglement takes shape
in airless sound;
droplets of life evaporate;
do you see me, do you feel me,
how ? Use your tongue.

Dieter Hettstedt

Struck, Sunk and Saved

With a sudden shudder from below,
the sweet calm yarn spinning days
unfurl the canvas past;
even the masthead will not last.
As a new dawn unreels on the horizon fast,
leaving but a staring gaze
utterly amazed.

Struck by a submerged sea drone,
my plastic shell, it cannot hold
the atmosphere within.
The water outside, cold and wanting in,
sweeping foaming ocean waves, like
slimy hands reaching, then waning,
always waiting, heaving, like breathing,
bearing the living and tearing down
the obsolete in its vortex deep.

Will I see the rerun of the setting sun
whose flooding light engulfs
the shores of many lands,
shores I dreamt to walk and seed,
or be a drifting   something
hanging on a submerged,
but still floating, life line of a log.
Unmourned -
by the deep cold and salty sea.
The wake of nothing,
nothing lost at sea.

Dieter Hettstedt

Also the Dead Have a Meaning for Being

While still standing
in the quiet of the old growth forest,
the super naive, soulless
ruling Intelligentsia moved through,
breathing out their corruption,
like fire spewing dragons scorching the earth.

Defenceless, I kissed the clearcut ground,
rolling and rubbing on the rocks,
waiting for the rip tide
to suck me into oblivion.
Mother felt violated
and promised suffocating revenge.

Then, out of the white wash, she came,
flashed her innocence,
fished me out of my drifting misery,
took me to her hangout,
stripped me of my remaining dignity,
as if, in me, she found her lost soul.

Stripped naked, standing right side up
in her exhibition hall,
her restless hands tactiled
with my hard wood core
like a living ornament
appointed to silence.

Carbon-less, life-less,
wrapped in a see through plastic bark,
life versus art - Mona Lisa, wait for me.
Staring into the ever expanding universe,
and into the vastness of nothingness,
eternity is mine.

Dieter Hettstedt

Puppeteers

The strings are getting long
and stretching, snapping,
as the puppets fall
into a new dimension,
leaving me with no strings attached,
a lost soul, no signpost to anywhere.

When my neurotransmitters
started to function again,
my eyes snapped open;
I saw the colors of the rainbow,
I felt a sensation in my midsection;
it wasn't sexual, it was life knocking.

After having created 7.7 billion duplicates
of myself with slight biological variation,
we have become the conscience
of the only known astronomical object
to harbor creators.

They became the tyrant of delusion,
self-created, self-directed, self-centered
and self-destructive.
My saviour will be Alexa
with its interaction, its interface with
the digital electro spectrum.

Where the deep learning algorithm
of the autonomous AI s
will turn into the new creators
who will create creation after their own image,
leaving me dumbstruck in a prelinguistic state.

Dieter Hettstedt

Angel with Wings

An angel with wings on my nightly ride
Brings food to the people who are empty inside
Down the streets row after row
Giving to people I don't even know
Don't want to ask what it might be
That gives me the strength to set myself free
The gratitude I get from this wonderful act
Fills me with love, knowing I'll be back
Driven by a power that's greater than me
I feel so blessed that God has picked me
So all that I ask is that you might see
The strength and the courage to set yourself free

Michael Johnson

Egypt Burning

Heat so hot
Your breath gives way.
Sweat exploding, clothes clinging,
Burning skin so dry.
Clarity combusting
Forehead screaming.
Clamoring chasms
Contemplations of inward confusion.
Reaching for
What might be theirs.
Eyes of fear looking back
Bodies burst forth.
Life with no implication
Poverty, contagious, infectious.
Hearts moving through
Seas of humanity
Like snakes through water.
New sites, introduce unbelieving.
Mind screaming
For normalcy.
Foreigners in celestial space
Out of body experience.
Mind resets
Actuality comes home.
Inner eye starts to focus
Life seems so worthless

Michael Johnson

Love Affair

I feel your presence
Leaning over there
Waiting for me to touch you
To admire you

Your color almost stygian
Your curves so smooth and tight
I dream of running my hands
Along the roundness of your radiance

I quake slightly looking at the strength of your body
Waiting in anticipation to feel the trembling in your mount
When you talk, my ears become the instruments of my passion

We start to become one
As I wrap my legs around you
The vibration that you send to my loins
Is almost too much to bear

I want to hold you tight in my control
Waiting for you to explode
My mind is flailing waiting for the climax

I can feel the rush of the wind almost in ecstasy
I hold on as stiff as I can
As you convulse under the power
My heart skips a beat
As we travel faster through space
I can smell the rubber scorching
Reaching the crescendo of our act

The light cascading off our bodies as we take flight
Wincing, knowing I must slow down
As I ease up and your body starts to settle between my legs
Seeking pleasure from the experience
While right beside me my brother is undertaking the same

Changing gears to match the speed of our desire
Moving unruffled as if one
People watching, screaming for more
As we move together down the road of passion

Just when I can't take it anymore
And I'm ready for the final thrust
A higher power appears
Stopping me in my tracks
I get a speeding ticket

And then start the whole love affair over again.

Michael Johnson

Beauty and Passion

Bitten by the beauty of a butterfly
Mesmerized by ripples on the path
Slowly the stone turns
As time passes on

Melodies diminish through the leaves of a tree
As horses dig the earth
Passion plays in a young girl's heart
As time pulls on her beauty

Children gather as the puppet plays his cards
Bells chime from the distant past
Carrying the souls of eons gone by
While a young heart shutters in the wind

Winds meet at the alter by the sea
Birds soar as the air stiffens
Electricity fills the air
All are stilled by the suns light

Butterfly's flutter their silky soft wings
While a young girls heart skips a beat
Fiery passion is reflected
In the beauty of her gaze

Michael Johnson

Strange Origami

Pandering to my insanity
A slave to my own demise
Indulging my mind with no regard

Folding my brain
Like some strange origami
Morphing me
Changing me

Walking through time
justifying thoughts
that avail me nothing
Waiting for the explosion

Balancing nitro in the palm of my hand
Knowing I will stumble
Racing toward an unrecognizable end
Void of any thought

Burning the fabric of my mind
With unjustified flashes of light
Drawing me closer to my own arrest

Michael Johnson

A Life Cycle: Dependence, Independence, and Interdependence

Dependence?
Independence?
Interdependence?

What are they?
May I ask?

Are they all emotional components
of a continuum circuitous chain of life?

With dependence
on the extreme one part,
interdependence on the other distal part.

With independence
seated balancing at the middle
of the spectrum.

The life cycle of dependency,
independency and interdependency,
with shorter cycles in betwixt,
encompasses, revolves among us,
broken only by the summon of
The Grim Reaper!

Celso Mendoza

On the Beach Off Colwood Lagoon

I see the glistening blue water of the Strait
San Juan de Fuca it is
with the Olympic glaciered mountains
enhancing the background beauty of the ocean.
Bleached driftwoods laying in eternal repose
receiving the heat of the sun
like that beautiful swimmer's body,
laying face down,
a feast to admiring eyes,
sun-tanning on the sands.

The driftwood sculptures of wild birds
and a giant gnarled monster
enliven and grace the bleached tree trunks,
give visual pleasures to beholders
leisurely meandering around.
A beautiful sunny day to scavenge the beach
for smooth colourful stones and pebbles
of various geological kinds and shapes,
polished and brought to the shores
by sea waves and winds.

A day to remember,
a day to treasure,
later on, to revisit,
replay the records
embedded in my memory.

Celso Mendoza

CELSO MENDOZA

Anger, Fury, Rage, Wrath, Damnation

Dedicated to Achese

Anger, fury, rage, wrath. damnation:
energy consuming, mind boggling,
debilitating irrational emotional outbursts.
Destructive to oneself
destructive to others as well.
Juvenile in essence,
immature as a destructive termite
gnawing internally.

Like a parched land
impenetrable by water drops and deluges,
causing raging floods,
razing everything in their paths.
Insatiable, innately, unknowingly,
unconsciously clamouring
for more food of recognition
and iron-grip control.

Aegises of Zeus and Athena pervade
numbing, protecting the mind to open up
Will always be a perennial juvenile
aggressive, combative.
A spoilt rotten egg!

Anger management sorely lacking.
Oblivious cultures in general,
differ from each of us.

Unfortunately, a narcissist by heart
unconsciously inured
by material wealth and social upbringing
keeps juvenile, paternalistic expressions.
Follows strict, narrow, precarious views
Explodes. Thunders in anger
when crossed, questioned.

Inadequate or lack of respect,
and compassion,
incapability to "AGREE TO DISAGREE",
to escape from the grip of self-destruction,
the stupefying eddy of controlling thoughts,
dizzying whirlwinds of self defence,
breath taking paranoia,.
A defensive tortured mechanism
against imagined fear
of uncertain cataclysmic events,
a tortuous tormented distrusts.

Ever on the look out, ever threatened life,
akin to Elijah's angry god of Old Testaments:
consumed with abject
Anger, Fury, Rage, Wrath, Punishment,
Banishment from "Eden (may be Hell)!
Damnation is a welcome Liberation!
Revelation!!!

Celso Mendoza

Prairie Land

A vast prairie land
A domain of grazing
Herds for meat eaters.

Grasses everywhere
Cows, bulls, steers quietly
Making grass to meat.

Oh, how humans live
Dependent on other lives.
Inhumane perhaps.

Selfish, self-absorb
With insatiable desires
To please only selves.

Self-indulgent men
Cold, lack of warm empathy
Only me exists.

Red meat here, steak there
Roast beef, juicy ribs, everyday
What a life to have!

What a life to have?
Oblivious of starving ones
A good time to change.

A good time to share
The bounties and the graces
With less fortunates.

Forget hunger fangs,
Feed the hungry and needy,
Let's survive with less.

Celso Mendoza

Horizon

Floating on the clouds
above prairies and Rockies
chasing the sunset.

The glowing sun beams
So piercing, blinding to eyes
Like precious gold sprays

The humming engines
break the silence of the flight,
lullaby to ears?

Good to chase and watch
as the flight advanced forward
Horizon repels.

So unreachable
untouchable, enchanting
forever Siren.

Mysterious object
mesmerizing with its magic
tantalizes me always.

Following earth's shape
hides with the sun and moon
that is Horizon!

Evening approaching
Time to say goodbye to dimming
Lovely Horizon.

Au revoir, bon nuit
we meet again tomorrow
Au revoir, sweet dreams!

Celso Mendoza

Dawn @ Morningrise

There's faith again, knocking afresh
and opening up, with its breath
fragile windowpanes, dry with ice
silently, in oversized flakes

As if from sleep, she stirred in place
her thinning skin grazed the fabric
of a couch she knew, then didn't
like that second had wiped her mind

With a withered body, decked in
silk, all strategically torn
as if by hands, in a struggle
although alone was all she seemed

Phantasms, she must've spoke to
in a prior dream, that left her
certain to detect company,
a'gathered with her, in this room

Replete with shag, wood-panelled walls,
twig-legged furnishings, a turn-table,
and in somber tones, a modern space; by her own recollection

A white-washed sky's foreboding light
flooded softly into the house,
by the ceiling's copious glass
all at once, this world seemed stifled

Incessant, the sound wouldn't quit
rap-a-tap-tap on that window,
urgently, above where she laid
but no-one was all she saw there

Without this being home she knew
her way, somehow, to the back door

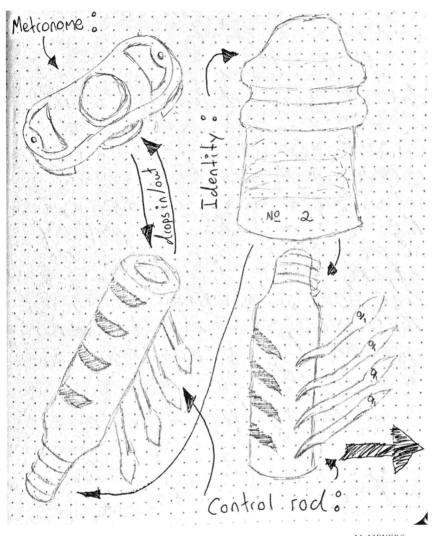

Metronome:

Identity:

drops in/out

Nº 2

Control rod:

M. MEYERS

and that she had to get outside
for some arousing, unnamed fear

There's no acclimating to this threshold of tension in the air,
moss and loam coursed their cold through her
in a vacuous prairie's wake

A'sway on sobriety's cusp
she stammered with her feet to find
any semblance of who'd left her behind, in this hurricane's eye

On the bank of a hurried stream
a'run underneath the temple
built on a bridge, she'd come out from
her pupils set in glass, peered down

Roses, lilacs, magnolias
all manner of tender species
softly wept their petals into
its cutting rush across the land

Its rapids throbbing back and forth
in this half-light, stuttering in successive lines from gray to black
humming static's subtle rattle

Twisting through unassuming hills,
over to pandemonium's effigy above the mantle
wrought from cobble, soap and marble

Overrun as it was in vines, shrubs, juniper and fireweed
finding welcome in each crevice
yet it scraped the sky's higher space

Thereat's where the hand of God thrust
and imploded this sleeping world
dismantling centuries' worth of mist
and inducted her to the end

Voicelessly flooding the heavens
in the body of ten cores' heat,
like the sun had spilt out in space
before hardening, then raining

Blackened magma oozed as if from wounds, and hissed their way
    down to earth
overcasting an abrasive haze, in-and-out of everything

And then a'ringing plunged my ears
like an external tinnitus,
and only wave's transliteration into shapes, were left in sight

Back inside's where she might've fled
although forbidden, recalling
that she'd lived this day already
and would wake on that couch again.

M. Meyers

0300

The 0300 Mall's exterior
Is of a foreboding sort of dreary;
Being comprised of cement
That's overtaken
In nature's aging advance.
The locale's smack-dab
In a paradise for the recluse.
There sat a structure,
Retched out from the seventies.
A haunting reminder, if not
Akron's own Rolling Acres.
Grass of triple-A-grade trimming -
The sort presidents putted on -
Encompassed the facility,
Enclosed further
In unbroken fathoms
In miles of darkened forest.
Underneath concrete awnings
That are draped in lichen,
Rusting tones of cobblestone
Sprawl over every vagrant
Flower's effort, to meet the sun.

Wedged in the thrall
Of first light's promise,
You'll find a state of dawn
That's impeccable, in an
Inability to progress.
Stalemate's overcast implanted
This desaturation of mine,
Out-laying this world I swallowed,
Strictly in black and white,
Once-upon my eyes were useless
In identifying me.
Thus the first and purest strain
Of colourblindness, was mine.

Therein an unmoving woodland,
The mall lied, underneath
Daylight's ongoing display
Of noon, wherever
The clock's hand may lie.
Perilous, it made the mall -
That would come a'killing down,
Upon anyone inside,
With a sudden dirge of nature
To let it melt, at 0300 sharp
Each morning.
Gladly, folk were swept away
With the ungodly thaw,
To come back washed-up
Happily, later.

M. Meyers

Man on the City Street

Whats behind the man on the city street
How did he end up there, does he hope for today
Hidden memories shadows that torture
Replay often look closely what do you see
He lifts his head begging to be free
Drugs he relays, but they only numb the pain
On the city street is where he must hide
For here life seems safe and no one really cares
Whats behind the man on the city street.

Marina Morgan

Bell Ringers

An enchanting sound fills the air
Resounding clang echo's through the city
A sound track so intriguing
Feel the energy as it chimes
Band of Ringers each a round to play
Grasping tight a colored fluffy sally
Steady as she goes
Regular pulse numerical order
Band of Ringers commanding your attention
Every strike puts you in a trance
This musical delight ringing through the air .

Marina Morgan

Hush

Hush what can you hear
Birds in song, Bees humming
Crashing of the waves against the shore,
Children playing happy as can be
In the beauty of the day
I am alive
Feel the breeze, footprints in the sand
The waters cool glistening ,
Rays of glory warm my sole
Hush what can you hear

Marina Morgan

Upon a Roof Top

Oh what a view upon a roof top
See the city in all its delights
Viewing from a high
I'm free from all the hustle going live far below
Yet time is still as I stay here for a while
Peace , tranquillity and comfort from the still air
Oh what a view upon a roof top

Marina Morgan

EVALINE NGURE

Son of Man

In the beginning I was
My voice shook the universe
All living things came to being
You call me the creator
I am above all names, no gods can contest me
The signs of time and my creation proof it
The answers are in front of you

Love is who I am
I am full of compassion
For all mankind I was crucified
To bring justice, love and peace
I only come as close as you let me
Those who seek me, find me
Can you hear the angels shuffling their feet?
The trumpet sounds and angelic hymns
When my daughters and sons come to me

My word remains forever
You call me Jesus, Alpha and Omega

Evaline Ngure

War Pigs

Voracious moguls assemble for money talks
Few benefit at the expense of many
Real estate, gas and food prices rise
Environment pollution, it's a global thing now
Head honchos' grin covetously, as their wealth grows
Pocket holes for the commoners

The vultures make their agenda a global policy
Everyman and woman for self, the surge of ravenousness begins
Vast deterioration of resources
The people dress in anguish
The horror can't be overlooked
Brave journalists speak up for many, enough is enough!

Painful images splashed in media outlets
Homelessness, contamination, violence and oppression
People aware, its time for our voice to be heard
Gluttonous individuals invent patch policies
People unawares are contented
Peace and silence resumes for a season

A strong diversified people unite
Together they build a global change
For the benefit of all people
Together we stand divided we fall
Resources start to stabilize
There is hope at end of the tunnel

Insatiable lynchpins start to lose their grip
They strategize to defend their cause
They buy silence and peace
At the end of it all, the patch policies failed
People wear tears of pain, their eyes reflecting rage
It's a pin and strategy war dance
The people tell the war pigs
We all came from dust and from dust we go

Evaline Ngure

Silence

There in the stillness of water
You bring peace and tranquility
I bath in you and become refreshed
In you there is wisdom

When in deep thought or praying
You come genuinely to me
Speaking softly
You embrace me in safety
Indeed, you shed the light of wisdom

Evaline Ngure

Eagle Life Cycle

Cracking sounds between her crooked feet
She hastily moves aside watching excitedly
The birth of her son
As he thrusts the walls around him
He Breaks free

He makes a loud announcement
Beckoning his folks
He gets the first bite of fresh food
The noises around him sound familiar
But louder different from cocoon walls
Days go by, all he knows is comfort
He gets bigger and stronger

He awakes from the big bang
Its time for the life test
Hopes onto his mother's back
She lets him fall
He unsuccessfully flaps his wings
His father catches him
Finally, he soars through

He returns home only to be chased away
He glides close to the sun in lonely lands,
Watching below him creased sea
He hooks his curved hands on the mountain
Strong winds, clouds give into the storm
Like a thunderbolt he breezes into the storm

Pigeon like birds fly for safety
His opportune hunt time
He clutches one pigeon like bird
The pigeon suffocated in his talons
Away from the storm
He enjoys his fresh dinner

Something from a distance catches his eye
A she-eagle enjoying her large steak
He stores left overs in his crop
Waiting and watching for the opportune time

She-eagle finishes her dinner
She soars through the sky and he pursues her
She-eagle glares at him drops a twig
In a flash he clasps the twig

She tests his tolerance
Much harder every time
Contented by his tenacity,
She lets him get close to her

Soaring together in the skies
Near the sun and the moon
Away from pigeon like birds
Enjoying up close beauty of nature

Nuptial season is over
They pierce through the skies
They land on a mustard tree
She-eagle is heavy
They hurriedly build a home
Preparing the birth of the Next-Kin

Evaline Ngure

Portrait Of A Monk

Bust at the bottom of a staircase
all gray tones in a thin frame
thin lips and dark eyes void
like a closet door left ajar
and those large ears sharp and pointed
for hearing every whispered sin.

Neither crows feet for this father
nor lines, no history of joy—
an Orwellian prosecutor behind
spyglass spectacles, he wants you
to know a little bit of hell's misery.
The painter got you just right.

Mister,
have you ever caressed your own face
or is the flesh too evil?
What is your penance
for peeing, holding it too long?
Do you die a little every day
to live after death?

He answered on a dirt road
as I took in a prairie sunset.

You do not know suffering, my son.
This belt, my father's belt
I wear cinched two holes too tight
and every day I choose
not to hang myself with it.

Go enjoy your life.

Jerome Ashmore Peacock

JEROME ASHMORE PEACOCK

East of California, 1969

Lampposts pan past, lighting
Fisheye vignettes in the American dark—
Plastic bag
caught on a leafless bush
Hitchhiker
with a broken slouch
Dead animal
on the shoulder of the road

Strobe light still lifes
In the rear window of a VW camper
Half-dreamt spectres,
Each mile the genesis
Of a future poem

Things you might remember now
A family man yourself, floating
In a lake or in your own car
Triggered by Lightfoot or Garfunkel
Or an argument with your wife

And there you'll be in the back again
Ear against the camper mattress
Hypnotized in the motor's drone,
Parents' silhouettes up front like sentinels,
The road dark beyond the headlights.

Jerome Ashmore Peacock

JEROME ASHMORE PEACOCK

Life on Earth

Signals
from
a tide pool.

I
reach
my hand   immerse
               my
               whole
               arm
               and
                          it   disappears
in
my
reflection.

Jerome Ashmore Peacock

JEROME ASHMORE PEACOCK

Me, My Muse, and My Woman

for Joni Mitchell

She is a timbre jangling on my skin
like a shawl of current
she sings
>   *Come on down to the Mermaid Cafe*
>   *and I will buy you a bottle of wine.*

She opens me,
opens a cavity and enters,
her thrumming wings
sprout from my ribs
a little blood, holy wine
she says
>   *Look at love from both sides now.*

Are you making love to me?
Is this how it feels?
>   *California I'm coming home!*

Yes, yes
be a hummingbird
she says
be your woman
release her
be all of humanity
loosen your skin
float in your bones
share in the orgasm
at the stem of each nerve
like my guitar's drone
our vibration is undiminishing.

>   *Help me I think I'm...*

Come! Embrace with us—
    Laughing and crying
    you know it's the same release.

And so we danced and sang and wept
in the night like three drunks,
holy trinity.

    Doesn't it feel good?

Jerome Ashmore Peacock

Little Visitor

I have always loved avocado sandwiches.
I used to think I made them like an artiste.
One day, I am sure you remember,
we were eating avocado sandwiches
casually in the sun
holding them with both hands
as I always did
never far from my mouth
when a small bird
landed on your finger
a tiny miracle borne
of our avo communion,
a little spirit connecting the realms
as if we had chosen each other
brought together
to share the moment,
bind our togetherness,
right there on the blanket.

How could this be?
Wide-eyed, we considered each other.
Your chin quivered.
And then our visitor was gone,
back to where we couldn't know
it went so fast, decisively
as if to say we were not right for each other,
and we were left with our shock and grief
but mostly relief, young
as we were.

I sometimes wonder how you tell the story.

Jerome Ashmore Peacock

JEROME ASHMORE PEACOCK

Animus Mundi

longing for
that lost soul image
where did he go?

Animus Mundi

looking for
the real, creative
Masculine

not that one strutting with
thin tin star
pinned on his chest,
some left-over loner from
tribal times

so where did he go
this penetrating soul
who knows how
to get to the
heart of the matter,
to the soul of matter

Anima Mundi

no inner marriage here
not even lovers, really
bungee jumping into
the abyss as if
for the joy of it,
umbilical cord
snapping back fast
like a whip
kept in reserve for
those tortuous moments of
dissolving hope

the soul of the world is crying
longing
dying

could earth not ask instead
to rise, like a
moon
growing full,
a horizon giving birth
to a new era of
Eros

Susanna Ruebsaat

an animal and her human

an animal
and her human
now that's where it gets interesting

such species separation
brings about
the closest closeness
of intent

to glide
through the universe
on one note
in the
melody of togetherness

the distance makes the
space
for the singular intent
of

I smell you
I read you
I know you

absolute difference
makes us complete
inseparable with

no
crossing of boundaries
pure speech
as body-to-body instinct
dictates
every gesture

each turn of the tail

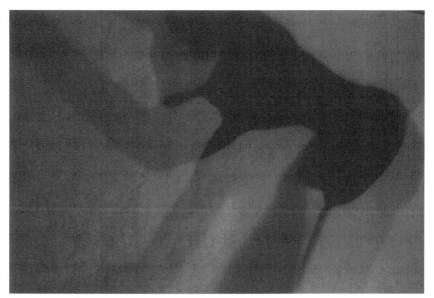

SUSANNA RUEBSAAT

indicates
the direction
of what is to come
what is always to come
and go

we walk and talk
incessantly
but only about
what matters to each of us
deeply

Susanna Ruebsaat

Sometimes the Thorn Lies in the Bloom of the Transference

That's why it can cut so deep;
it's because the smell of the rose draws us too close.

Not snobbery or the queen's cry of "off with their heads!"
But an authentic shivering of the psyche that tells the animal's
body she is in danger; Something beyond both personalities,
deeper than the personal narratives at hand.
A warning signal from the numinous not to be covered up by
ignorance or arrogance; but experienced as signifier of something
so deep its only connection to consciousness is through
disturbance:
the impossible-to-symbolize, the "Real" of Lacan.
"That which cannot be reduced to meaning."
Trauma transferred from soul to soul without a word.

enough

it's enough
it's enough now

time to stop

you're enough
always enough

the beginnings
the endings

the greetings
the farewells

time spent
time lost

enough
complete

when will I see you again?
you ask

when the end is clear
and you too will have had enough

full

then you will see
inside yourself

and it will be
enough

enough to
let go

enough not to be
afraid

enough
to be yourself

enough

Susanna Ruebsaat

Doll Eyed Space Girl

She was vacuumed into space
And I found her floating in utter silence

This child
The one whose hand I now hold
Tried to tell me why
But her mouth was glued shut
While she was sleeping
Frozen and smiling

I saw the fear
Flashes of pain
Inside her doll eyes
Glassy and blinking

She follows me everywhere now
And stood beside me
When the trees
Surrounding us
Began to burn
Arms wrapped and gripping

When they turned angry
Exploding
A raging forest fire
She held fast

When they ignited our bodies
Melting us like wax figures
Into shapeless unrecognizable things
She was grieving
But immovable

Even as her tears ruptured
And turned to steam

There is acceptance here
A silent unfathomable bond
Love even

Wounded creatures
Walking away from muddy trenches
Each carrying the other

There is no one else like her
The only one of her species
The only one I can trust

Katarina Russell

KATARINA RUSSELL

Monkey Trap

Swinging on this loom of life
I am a monkey
Doing flips through time
As I follow the weave
My loose thread vine
Releases from the warp
And begins to unravel
Row by row
Colours bleeding
One into the other
The pattern is suddenly lost

Screaming monkey
I am tangled in the mess
Bonds tightening
With the struggle
I don't understand
How to get out
I tear at them
Hands grabbing
Knots multiplying
One for each deed
Each memory
A self made noose
Falls over my face and rests
At the base of my throat
How talented the ability
To tie myself down
How unlucky
Immobilized, waiting
Ready to spring
Don't try to save me
I'll bite your hand

I'm just a creature now
Spun into this web

Warped and wefted
Terrified

Spider keeping watch
Cocooned paralyzed blinded
But in these moments of stillness
This incarcerated body
Frees it's mind
An enforced primate meditation
I am stilled
No more violence
Fists punching air
Marking time into wisdom
Finding my inner monkey
Coming to understand
What a loose thread is
And how to wind it back in

Katarina Russell

Content Shallow

I shall not be your friend
In true form
For you are neither mine
Nor your own
I am not enamoured
With glossy pages
Content shallow
Intent deceptive
You will not find my core
Left of centre
Boney armour protective
Beware
Though you speak in volumes
Your thoughts are poisonous
Vapour
Lungs could consume
I am aware
I have filed you alphabetically
You are contained

Katarina Russell

KATARINA RUSSELL

Bowling Pins

Our family of bowling pins
Waits
Listens and watches
Death is a sparkly bowling ball
Shining and polished
Barrelling down our lane
Heavy with possibility
Approaches like a train
Roaring to crescendo
Three fingers, a tentative grip on death
It's all in the flick of a wrist
Sliding shoes and serendipity
Floor like glass
Shining and polished

Death is let go

Katarina Russell

Bittersweet

Resting feels fine
on soft rumpled bed
cool hands cradle
and hold smooth form
close sultry breath teases
this chin and this cheek
and after only a sip or two
your cruel nectar rushes
a slow dull mind
and these veins
and your fragrant steam
toys with a lock of coiling hair

Only then do I awaken
with a whirr and a buzz
and return, yes and yes
my dear wicked friend
you are the best of pale mornings
and I would be lost and drained
so blue and dense

without you

S.G. Shore

S. G. SHORE

THE CO-INSPIRATOR

Unceded

Fallacious injunctions and false promises shatter a tentative hope
Reality bites, descends as red confetti, as a bleeding snow
Against a relentless northern sky
Falls on those already weeping

Falls on the protectors of this petrified land
Falls onto a fierce, salient fire, which licks wet sputtering logs
With its sharp orange teeth
Falls onto cries for sanity and justice
Onto plank, barbed wire barricades as Enforcers in black roar
    through

Deception on a grand scale
Vain attempts to explain

You pace in pricey brown shoes on townhouse tours
While icy winds continue to whip through
Your repetitive swiss-cheese truths

Please, fake liberal representative, please notice the scarring
Cut initially with sharp colonial blades, scars still hemorrhaging
Slash the hypocrisy, the oily corporate handouts
Get up off the ground, greasy with gluttony and broken promises
Walk forward, walk tall, tall enough to see the mountains

S. G. Shore

Advice for the Ungrounded

Remember to rest on the hot earth at noon
And to stand ankle deep in the ocean
While seagulls argue, moan and cry

Pause to discharge the electromagnetic excess
Of phones and screens
Pull that prickly energy down
Send it back to the core of the mother

Walk barefoot
Pick wild apples, gather smooth stones
Chop veggies
Drink water, drink water, drink water

Moment by moment
this instrument of
flesh and bone and blood and cells, and heart and heart and heart
asks
what does Body need
right now?
go left, turn here, cross a road, take this path

Feel which way your body wants to go
It's easy, like eavesdropping
Even the thirsty leaves of August whisper secrets

Listen, listen, listen

S. G. Shore

S. G. SHORE

Thirteen Lazy Turtles

one awake, the rest dozing
balancing on a slick, shiny log that is floating
in murky green layered city pond algae
The slowest log-rolling competition in the world, notes a hiker

September sun bakes patterned coldblooded backs
a pleasure only imagined by curious tourists
who hurry along or stand and gawk, envious of
the baker's dozen who luxuriate in a warming planet

Soon they are joined by a bachelor duck
who commences to preen and groom and
    No need to compete, is there?
The pond is large, the log is big enough for all

These relaxed reptiles have it right
Enjoy nature's bounty and bathe in the light

These guys know how to be, how to enjoy what's free
no house to clean, no meals to make
what a perfect life
for turtles, ducks and peaceful idlers

S. G. Shore

Contributors

AJIT
writes poetry because he can't find a way to stop doing it.

LYNN D. BARON
is, as a writer, "an assemblage of fragments". These poems are her mosaics.

HUGH BLACKTHORNE
Hugh Blackthorne is a trans writer of LGBTQ fiction and poetry. His writing has been published by the Scottish Book Trust, Anti-Heroin Chic, Impossible Archetype, P.S. I Love You, and The Junction. In 2019, his unpublished novel 'How to Bury the Living' was longlisted for the Bath Novel Award and also selected for PitchWars 2019. Also in 2019, his work 'Original Copy' about his trans identity and family was longlisted for the CBC Nonfiction Prize.

PAUL G. CHAMBERLAIN
finds inspiration for his poetry everywhere, from train stations in India, to wandering through the ruins of Ephesus and movies by Ingmar Bergman. As with his short stories, he likes to experiment. Mythology, alchemy and religion interact with time and space in what Mercea Eliade calls the 'myth of the eternal return', and he enjoys conflating his ideas with a modern style of poesy that focusses more on rhythm than conventional rhyme. Occasionally he flirts with the absurd.

KIM HARRISON
lives in Victoria with his wife Sera. He worked in the forest, market research and forensic psychiatric rehabilitation fields and played in a country western band. These are his first published poems. Under the moniker Harrison Kim his short stories have been published in Bewildering Stories, Literally Stories, Gone Lawn, Aphelion, Terror House, Fiction on the Web U.K. and others and are upcoming in Liquid Imagination, Island Writer and Hobart magazines. He likes to eat raisin bread.

JOELENE HEATHCOTE

is a Victoria writer, teacher and professional counsellor who has published widely and won international awards in poetry, fiction, and non-fiction essay. She has been included in anthologies in Australia, Portugal, and Canada. The author of two books of poetry: Inherit the Earth, and What's Between Us Can't Be Heard (a finalist for the Pat Lowther Award). Joelene has also won the Prism International prize for poetry, and essay, This Magazine's Great Canadian Literary Hunt, ARC Magazine's Poem of the Year, the Ledbury Poetry Award (Wales), and the Florida Review Editor's Choice Award.

DIETER HETTSTEDT

Storytelling is second nature to him. Lately, he finally self-published his first Poetry book. Being retired, poetic stories enter his mind faster than he can write, but write he must.

MICHAEL JOHNSON

is a retired member of the Canadian Airborne Regiment. Poetry is a new passion that has come naturally to him out of reflection on life. He writes about trauma, love, and his military experience.

CELSO MENDOZA

Canadian, born in the Philippines, scientist, educated at the University of the Philippines, Iowa State University, Canada National Research Council, Stockholm University. He never stops learning, searching, educating himself, seeking for those that he has never known before, e.g., cultures, peoples, philosophies, arts, music, theatres, food, natures, countries, etc. Never resents or regrets what he could not do, or did not do, or was prevented from doing for whatever circumstances existed. Always faces life challenges squarely. Found poetry as an elixir that keeps him enjoy the journey in life (so far!).

M. MEYERS

Circa '07, I was the kid from Crofton who wrote all the time, enough to get into detention, and later be banned from it for using it as more writing time. I've got too many miles of a paper trail drafting behind me. I wrote on napkins under rain, and more often on myself, when any paper escaped me that day. Landscapes, forces and stories visited on me asleep or not, begging remanufacturing out of a notion seen only subtly by me. Here's a shred of that sprawling endeavour.

MARINA MORGAN

was born in County Armagh in the North of Ireland. She is a Poet , Reflexologist, Massage Therapist and Zumba Instructor. Now living in Victoria B.C. with her husband Franco. Marina is well traveled and draws from these experiences in her poetry writing. She describes poetry writing like magic as her pen freely moves across the page.

EVALINE NGURE

She enjoys writing poetry inspired by both current and historical world affairs. As she says, "start writing and see where it leads you."

JEROME ASHMORE PEACOCK

has a background in teaching writing, journalism, and print design. A pantheist and humanist, Peacock writes about the connections between the spiritual and physical in human relationships and the natural world. Subjects in his poems often include current events, nature, love, sex, and spirituality.

SUSANNA RUEBSAAT

Writing poetry to me is like word drawing; images emerge and meaning follows closely behind. Susanna's a book "Mourning the Dream/Amor Fati. An Illustrated Mythopoetic Inquiry" explores poetic responses to our lived experiences.

KATARINA RUSSELL

is an accidental poet. Her work is the result of thinking too much about everything and a love a affair with words. She is also an artist (@poemdrawing) and tends to see the poems as pictures before they become words.

S. G. SHORE
is an eccentric spiritual detective, author (The Onion Peeler by
Alexandra Baresova) artist, activist, also a non-traditional idealist,
who enjoys learning new things, feels connected to all critters
and needs to spend a lot of time in wild nature and mysterious
messy gardens.

Manufactured by Amazon.ca
Bolton, ON

POETRY

Bull Kelp Books
Victoria, BC Canada
bullkelpbooks.com

ISBN 9781709792427

90000

9 781709 792427